MARISSA KEVINS

EMOTIONAL DISORDER

The Ultimate Guide on How to Fight Depression, Discover the Steps and Effective Ways on How to Cope With Depression and Melancholic Tendencies

Descrierea CIP a Bibliotecii Naţionale a României
MARISSA KEVINS
EMOTIONAL DISORDER. The Ultimate Guide on How to Fight Depression, Discover the Steps and Effective Ways on How to Cope With Depression and Melancholic Tendencies / Marissa Kevins – Bucharest: Editura My Ebook, 2020
ISBN

MARISSA KEVINS

EMOTIONAL DISORDER

**The Ultimate Guide on How to Fight Depression,
Discover the Steps and Effective Ways on How to
Cope With Depression and Melancholic Tendencies**

My Ebook Publishing House
Bucharest, 2020

TABLE OF CONTENTS

Foreword

Are you blue, anxious, irritable, tired, inundated or emotionally delicate? These forms of mood disorders have become shockingly common, and in a lot of cases, may easily be resolved.

Depression and anxiety particularly have become so prevalent that it's exceedingly common for individuals to be taking medication for one or even both of these mood disorders. As a matter of fact, the incidence of depression and anxiety has tripled since 1990 and more than twenty-five percent of the adult population in the U.S. suffers from one or more mood troubles.

Defeat Depression!

Ways to cope with depression and melancholic tendencies.

CHAPTER 1

JOURNALING

Synopsis

Occasionally depression or a blue mood might have no evident cause and occasionally it might be caused by a number of elements. Keeping a journal is among the most potent tools available for personal growth and emotional mending. It may and should be a day-to-day ritual. Putting down our views lets us view them as separate from ourselves.

Writing

Once a thought is no longer perceived as a facet of your identity, it's conceivable to question it. When an idea is mistaken for truth it may be hard to pull out from under the feelings affiliated with that idea. For instance, an individual who is newly divorced may think, "I'll be alone eternally as no one will love me ever again." This is likely not true, but the idea may seem so big and true and undeniably real, that it absorbs the entire sense of self. Feelings of aloneness and desperation become profoundly rooted and depression sets in for the long run.

Journaling exclusively might not ease depression, However it may help lift it and relax its grip. Day-to-day journal practice has the might to radically alter your life. Be unafraid. Bringing out of depression is worth it.

Some ideas to get you going:

➤ Once you get out of bed do a little stretching, yoga, or exercise to get the blood running for five-ten minutes.

➤ Drink some water (add a little lemon juice). Dehydration aggravates feelings of depression and tiredness. Citrus aromas have a mildly intoxicating quality and lemon helps detoxify the liver.

➤ Make certain your writing area is clean and comfy. Set a timer for a quarter-hour and get seated.

➤ The sole rule is that you must keep writing for the entire quarter-hour. Put down anything and everything that comes into your head. If you get stuck, write your to-do list, or a nice memory, anything. Just don't quit moving your hand.

➤ When time's up close your notebook and don't look at what you wrote for a few weeks, at least. Make certain you keep your notebook someplace that no one may by chance read it. This material isn't meant to be read, it's meant to be composed.

➤ Do this every day.

Here is another exercise that can be done anytime; Many times a day if you feel overly negative you may begin a blog to share your gratitude with the world.

Simply put down at the least five things that are great in your life. You may begin each one with "I'm thankful for..." or "I'm thankful because..." Do you have your health? Something to be thankful for.

Was there a fresh gentle wind this daybreak? When you get going you'll be astonished at how much you've to be thankful for. This type of journaling has a potent calming effect on the soul.

CHAPTER 2

WELLNESS CHECKLIST

Synopsis

A wellness checklist ought to handle the needs of mind, body, and soul by rendering honest daily goals. It's meant to encourage you as you battle depression, not drown you, so keep it easy.

Be Well

Stick with an individual page. Utilize a "friendly" font in an easy-to- read size. If black-and-white is too stark, try out a typeface in a calming color. Print a fresh copy of the list every day.

If you're truly fighting to battle depression, your list might include the barest of daily chores -- the very matters we do without thinking when we're feeling fine. Get up in the morning, shower, and Brush my teeth might need to go to at the beginning of your list. You'll likely feel goofy initially, marking off such everyday chores. The thought is to remind yourself that you are able to battle depression by attending to yourself in the commonest ways.

The accompanying things will assist you in making your every day checklist.

- ➢ Awaken with a mental attitude of gratitude and think about what I'm thankful for
- ➢ Exercise
- ➢ Consume a sound breakfast
- ➢ Take my vitamins
- ➢ Consume healthy snacks
- ➢ Stimulate my brain
- ➢ Drink enough water
- ➢ Love somebody or serve somebody today
- ➢ Get five-seven servings of veggies
- ➢ Crawl in bed at a time that will let me get enough sleep

Here is an illustration of another type of checklist. You are able to Print this page or make one the way you prefer for yourself.

1. I recognize my greatest tension triggers. Tension triggers:

2. I've somebody to talk to or a place to write, when my tension level is elevated.
   My contact individuals are:

3. I've a way to unwind. Restful activities:

4. I consume an assortment of foods and get the nutrients I require. I have healthy food available.
   Sound foods I enjoy:

5. There have been no big shifts in my appetite recently. Name any alterations or state no alteration:

6. I take part in some form of physical activity. Physical activities and how often:

7. I'm acquiring decent sleep. There have been no big alterations in my sleep habits recently.
   List sum of sleep/alterations:

9. I'm involved in sociable activities. My sociable activities include:

10. I've enlightened my family and loved ones about my illness to the best of my power.

List of resources or tips to help:

CHAPTER 3

KEEP NUTRITION IN CHECK

Synopsis

Beneficial nutrition is crucial when you need to battle depression. This is tricky, as depression tends to cut off the appetite. In order to battle depression, you need to take up enough calories and nutrients to provide your body and brain strength.

Eat Right

Cooking a meal might be an intimidating chore while you're depressed, and it'll appear senseless if you're not interested in eating. If you make healthy eating as simple as possible, you'll not only battle depression, you'll be better able to reject junk food. Sugar highs and the crashes that unavoidably follow will only make you feel sorrier.

Battle depression by purchasing healthy, likable foods that call for little or no cooking: soups, fruit, cheese, yogurt, whole - grain cereal, and so forth. If you can't pull off eating full meals, you are able to still get a great portion of the calories you require daily from nourishing snacks and light meals. If you tend to scarf out when depressed, better to have the healthy sundries around for eating. You'll be less likely to get hold of the box of doughnuts.

A lot of the symptoms of depression may be directly linked to vitamin and mineral inadequacies in the standard diet, which is mostly made up of hollow carbs, caffeine and sugar. Depression, mood swings and weariness often have a basic cause: pitiful nutrition. Quashing depression or recovering from a depressive sequence is frequently as simple as altering your diet and boosting your intake of key foods that have brain-boosting nutrients and help govern brain chemistry.

Fish oils bear omega-3s. Research has demonstrated that depressed individuals often lack a fatty acid called EPA. Just a gram of fish oil each day can bring a 50% reduction in symptoms like anxiety; sleep disorders, unexplained feelings of sorrow, self-destructive thoughts, and diminished sex drive. Omega-3s tare found in walnuts, flaxseed and oily fish like salmon or tuna fish.

18

Another top food for delivering imega-3 fatty acids is chia.

Brown Rice holds vitamins B1 and B3, and folic acid. Brown rice is likewise a low-glycemic food, which means it frees glucose into the bloodstream bit by bit, forestalling sugar lows and mood swings.

Instant forms of rice don't offer these benefits. Any time you see "instant" on a nutrient label, avoid it.

Brewer's Yeas bears vitamins B1, B2 and B3. It should be avoided if you don't stomach yeast well, but if you do, mix a thimbleful into any smoothie for your every day dose. This super food has sixteen amino acids and fourteen minerals. Amino acids are critical for the nervous system.

Cabbage holds ascorbic acid and folic acid. Cabbage protects against tenseness, infection and heart conditions. There are a lot of ways to get cabbage into your diet; like salad, wraps, stir fry and classic cabbage soup.

Foods like raw cacao, dark molasses and Brazil nuts are likewise excellent for annihilating depression.

If you're depressed you likewise need to quash particular foods and substances. You should avoid caffeine, smoking and foods high in fat and sugar. Maintaining your blood sugar and acquiring B vitamins is crucial for stabilizing your mood.

CHAPTER 4

ADEQUATE SLEEP

Synopsis

Sleep furnishes the armor you require to battle depression. Without enough rest, you're more susceptible to those damaging messages twirling around in your brain, and less able to do beneficial things on your own behalf.

Rest

If you're fighting with insomnia, make certain your bedroom is made for sleep. It should be an area for rest, not stimulus. Do away with anything related to work and additional sources of concern, like paperwork and bills. If you keep a TV set or computer in your room, move it someplace else. Battle depression by making the minutes prior to sleep as peaceful as imaginable.

Once it's time to switch off the lights, cover digital clocks - those beaming numbers that keep you perpetually mindful of how late it's getting, and of how much sleep you're lacking. Do your best to bar all light sources; the goal is to produce a space of pitch blackness.

Individuals who are exhausted feel more aggression and moodiness and are more prone to get depression and anxiety.

An occasional insomniac night generally isn't much of an issue, but running a sleep shortage over time may cause many problems. Every system in your body is impacted by deficiency of sleep.

Determine why you're having troubles sleeping. Tension, depression and anxiety may be the cause and to settle the problem, these issues have to be confronted. Sleep apnea might be causing you to partly awaken before REM sleep has happened, leaving you open-eyed and fatigued.

It may be something easy too. You might need a fresh mattress or to discover a way to dim the room better. Noises might be keeping you awake, so "white noise" might be required. It may very well be all of the above.

Some individuals will need medical intervention. Serious depression and anxiety should be cared for by the doctor. As for sleep apnea, a sleep study ought to be done, so the best resolution may be determined. There are a lot of answers, ranging from a splint to keep your jaw moved forward to particular breathing masks.

Herbal answers for stress might be of value. Kava Kava is a beneficial choice. It can't be taken on a steady basis, and you shouldn't drive when taking it. Longer term herbs include lavender, chamomile, passionflower and jasmine. For insomnia itself, valerian and hops might be of value. Mild to moderate depression might be alleviated with St. John's Wort. However, make certain you wear sunscreen as that herbaceous plant may cause you to suit photosensitive.

Attempt and set up a steady routine - Go to bed and rise at approximately the same time daily. No TV or reading when you go to bed. If you're a coffee drinker, make certain it's not more than a cup or two in the morning exclusively. Getting regular physical exercise may be a big help in getting more sleep. If you're sleep deprived, try your downright hardest not to nap during the day. All this does is mess up your sleep pattern.

The human body demands rest, and once you discover what is keeping you from the sleep that you require, the better off you'll be.

CHAPTER 5

EXERCISE EVEN THOUGH IT'S DIFFICULT

Synopsis

A lot of studies have determined that exercise and activeness may greatly help relieve the symptoms of depression and help better the quality of life for individuals who suffer from depressive disorder. Although the precise reasons why exercise has a favorable impact on depression aren't clear-cut, the findings are bright.

Get Moving

Exercise that calls for the utilization of big muscle groups might help relieve the feelings of "repressed" anxiety. Moving, stretching the muscles, the freedom of full-range of motion, and increasing circulation, and so forth, might help persons release tension and hostility. Exercise betters one's physical body, weight and total appearance. This may certainly help improve one's mood through heightened self-esteem and confidence. Persons who exercise frequently feel better as they feel they're in control of themselves, their body and thus, their lives. A sense of mastery accompanies the improved self-esteem exercise furnishes. Exercise has been shown to produce beta-endorphins, the body's own morphine-like painkillers and source of euphoria. This "feel good" sensation is much cited as "runner's high".

Exercise is becoming a more accepted form of therapy. Some of the advantages of exercise in depression are as follows:

1. Individuals have reported that, when they exercise, may think more clearly, feel happy, feel better about themselves, slim down, develop strength, and enjoy a sense of welfare.

2. Exercise expanded positive mood

3. They rest better

4. Get less jitteriness and anxiety,

5. Exercise diminished negative mood

6. Exercise bettered vigor

7. Exercise might help in increasing the feelings of coherency

8. Exercise increased the feelings of social integration

Exercise may be as good as and even more beneficial than prescription pills in addressing depression. The cause for this is because exercise has utterly no side effects, in fact it brings with it a number of health advantages. Furthermore, the positive effects of it on the brain are apparent as soon as the first workout is done.

Exercise discharges the natural pain killers of the body, namely the epinephrine and the nor-epinephrine which are likewise known to act as mood-boosters.

You can run, kick box, spin or skip rope, as each of these is high on intensity. If running is a bit much for you, you can begin with walking and slowly promote yourself to a brisk walk and then maybe, to a slow jog.

When you're brisk walking make certain your mind is alert. Be alert of your breathing, the natural environment and the sensations of your body. A state of alert ease will help you in battle anxiety and depression. It will better mental clarity and make you more cognizant of your surroundings.

It's true that the very beginning day of your workout is going to be demanding as your body isn't used to it. But if you're still tired after a week's exercise, something isn't right with your routine. Get professional assistance as an unsound exercise routine is worse than none.

Make certain you eat something healthy before beginning to exercise. A whole fruit, a few crackers or a glass of milk are beneficial ideas.

Never exercise on an empty tummy as that may step-up your depressive episodes.

CHAPTER 6

DON'T DRINK

Synopsis

Equal to 40 % of individuals who drink heavily have symptoms that resemble a depressive sickness.

All the same, when these same individuals are not drinking heavy, only 5% of men and 10% of woman have symptoms fitting the diagnostic standards for depression - not that different from the ranges of depression in the general population.

Don't Do It

Approximately 5 to 10%of individuals with a depressive illness likewise have symptoms of an alcohol issue.

Both alcohol troubles and depression are exceedingly common. They might occur conjointly or completely independently. Individuals with depression occasionally utilize alcohol as a form of self-medication, for instance either in an endeavor to cheer themselves up, or occasionally to help them sleep. While in small quantities alcohol may briefly elevate mood, if used to try to cope with a depressive illness, troubles come up. Whether taken to address a depression or not, it produces a downer effect on people's mood.

Depression may lead to thoughts of suicide. The lack of self- discipline, compromised judgment and impulsivity from the alcohol may increase the chances of an individual attempting suicide.

Typically, a much greater incidence of suicide, both completed and attempted, is affiliated with alcohol.

The basic problems of depression and alcohol are often complicated by social troubles. Alcohol may often lead to problems at work in the form of absenteeism, illness and under functioning. The loss of an occupation has a heavy negative impact on an individual's financial condition and family life. Marital troubles frequently arise because of an alcohol issue, although it might be difficult to say which began first.

Alcohol may also induce a big number of physical problems. Few, if any organs in the body are spared. Liver troubles generally arise from heavy alcohol intake and may take the form of jaundice resulting from hepatitis, cirrhosis of the liver or liver failure. Uncurbed these will lead to death.

A few antidepressants are tranquilizing. If they're taken with alcohol, an individual can be severely sedated and at risk of their breathing ceasing. To boot, numerous antidepressants are broken down in the liver. Because alcohol may damage the liver, the levels of these antidepressants in the body will be greater in individuals who are also drinking heavy. This may lead to an increase in side effects from the antidepressants.

A lot of the symptoms reported by individuals drinking heavily resemble those of depression like:

➤ Tiredness
➤ Interrupted sleep
➤ Early morning rousing
➤ Inadequate energy levels
➤ Inadequate appetite.

The state of affairs is further complicated as heavy alcohol intake may lead to depression. As a result, its normal practice to deal with the alcohol issue first and see if the depression gets better. If it doesn't, then particular treatment for the depression would be started.

Treatment with a selective serotonin reuptake inhibitor (SSRI) antidepressant may better both depression and an alcohol issue. This might point towards a common cause for both disorders.

CHAPTER 7

DON'T BLAME YOURSELF

Synopsis

We all have bad or damaging thoughts at onetime or another in our lives, but if foul thoughts are recurring and touching on you seriously then you need to take action to control your focus.

Be Kind

Ceaseless worry, doubt or negativism may be caused from mental illness like depression. It may also deduce from side effects of a medicine, diet or from being extremely stressed. If your way of thinking is impacting how you act around other people by altering your mood and behavior, then you need to assess what could be at the core of the issue. Once you're able to ascertain you've a problem you should troubleshoot to discover the best solution for you. When it comes to containing a mental behavior you must keep in mind that what works best for some individuals might not work for you.

Defeating depression is difficult, maybe the most difficult thing you'll ever do. Opposing depression isn't a stroll in the park; it's a dogfight. But if you choose to join the fight, you can win the struggle. Your emotions are an expression of your thoughts. When you alter your ideas, your emotions automatically alter. You don't have to fight the negative and bent emotions repeating in your brain. Rather, you need to learn how to alter the way you think, and emotions will by nature take care of themselves. Like dark follows daylight, when your views are healthy and favorable, your emotions become healthy and favorable as well.

If you would like to alter the way you feel, you're going to have to alter your inner dialogue. You're going to have to talk to your brain in a different manner. You in reality push your brain in a positive direction by putting favorable and healthy thoughts into your mind.

If you put enough favorable thoughts into your mind, you are able to actually produce a positive mind. You're not lost, and your life isn't hopeless. Your life instantly improves the minute you begin putting beneficial things into your mind. The fight against depression is fought on the battleground of focus. In order to break the back of depression, you'll have to learn how to persistently and consistently command the focus of your mind.

When you alter the things you view, the way you view things changes. When you alter the things you discuss, the way you discuss things changes. When you alter the things you consider, the way you consider things changes. It truly does matter what you view, what you discuss, and what you consider, because all of these things alter who you are and make you into a different individual. You must view positive things, discuss positive things, and consider positive things if you would like to be free from depression and become a positive individual.

Depressed individuals skillfully brush off the facts; they pass over them and go directly to their feelings. Once they totally engulf themselves in their feelings, they invent "facts" that are consistent with those feelings. For all pragmatic purposes, they think backward.

You must no more think that you're what you feel. Rather, you turn the law around and say that the facts of life determine the feelings of life. You become an authority at ferreting out the facts and making a point that your feelings are ordered with them. If the feelings aren't correct, you ignore your feelings and go with the realities till your feelings change.

CHAPTER 8

SEE SOME ONE

Synopsis

Cognitive behavioral therapy (or CBT) is a psychotherapeutic plan of attack that aims to solve troubles concerning dysfunctional emotions, behaviors and cognitions by a goal- oriented, systematic process. The title is utilized in various ways to specify behavior therapy, cognitive therapy, and to refer to therapy based on a combination of common behavioral and cognitive research.

Get Help

There are empirical grounds that CBT is efficient for the treatment of an assortment of troubles, including mood, anxiety, personality, eating, drug abuse, and psychotic disorders. Treatment is frequently done with particular technique-driven brief, direct, and time-limited treatments for particular mental disorders. CBT is utilized in individual therapy as well as group scenes, and the strategies are frequently altered for self-help applications. A few clinicians and researchers are more cognitive oriented, while others are more behaviorally pointed. Other intercessions combine both.

Before going for the cognitive therapy you need to recognize the advantages of cognitive therapy in addressing depression. Will it help you to bring out of depression? The cognitive therapy may work in a lot of different ways. Firstly it supplies the depressed individual with a supportive counseling. This helps to ease the hurt of depression.

With the assistance of this therapy the feeling of hopelessness is likewise addressed. Overall it has some capital effects on the minds of the depressed individual.

During depression the individual seems to get pessimistic. The therapy helps to alter the pessimistic thoughts as well as the unrealistic expectations. Occasionally critical self evaluation may likewise cause depression. This therapy may even help you out of that.

This therapy helps the individual to realize the troubles of life which are severe as well as minor. The therapy works to formulate the positive goals of life and helps the individual to
36

value himself positively. The advantages of cognitive therapy in depression have been recognized by most psychiatrists.

Some cognitive tips you can do on your own:

The act of writing automatically puts some space between you and your damaging thought. Jotting things down allows for perspective and helps individuals detect malformed thinking more easily. If you're in a situation where you just can't put pen to paper, it's recommended stating things aloud.

Figure out what's truly bothering you? Is it merely the fact that you got a flat? Or is it that you dirtied your outfit while changing it? Or that you knew you required a new tire but didn't replace it?

You may feel annoyed about the flat, disappointed that replacing it dirtied your outfit, furious at yourself for not replacing it in time. So identify the damaging themes. About failing to replace the tire: "I forever stall. I never take care of matters in time." About dirtying the outfit, "I'm a pig. I can't go anyplace and look alright."

Next discover distortions and replace rational reactions.

"I don't always stall. I juggle my occupation and loved ones and execute just about everything that has to get done. "I'm not a pig. I'm generally really careful about my appearance, more so than most individuals, which is why affairs like this upset me.

Next reconsider the problem.

Are you still heading for and emotional frenzy? Likely not. But you still feel peeved about getting the flat.

Finally plan corrective action.

"As soon as I get off work, we're getting that tire. That will take the time I've planned to spend cooking dinner, so I have gather up some take-out as an alternative."

Wrapping Up

Depression might be among the worst illnesses we know, but it's highly treatable. Discovering what works might involve weeks or months - and occasionally even years - of frustration and heartbreak, but with the range of options we now have, your prospects are excellent. Furthermore, we're not helpless bystanders. The decisions we make affecting our lifestyles can dramatically better the odds in our favor. To those of you, who are depressed, please look for help - you shouldn't have to hurt one day longer than you have to. For those of you fighting with your treatments don't give up hope. A more brilliant future lies ahead.

Printed by Libri Plureos GmbH in Hamburg, Germany